THE EVER-GROWING VINE ON MY WINDOW

PARNIKA CHANDRA

notionpress.com

INDIA · SINGAPORE · MALAYSIA

ISBN

Hardcase 979-8-89588-998-5

Paperback 979-8-89588-336-5

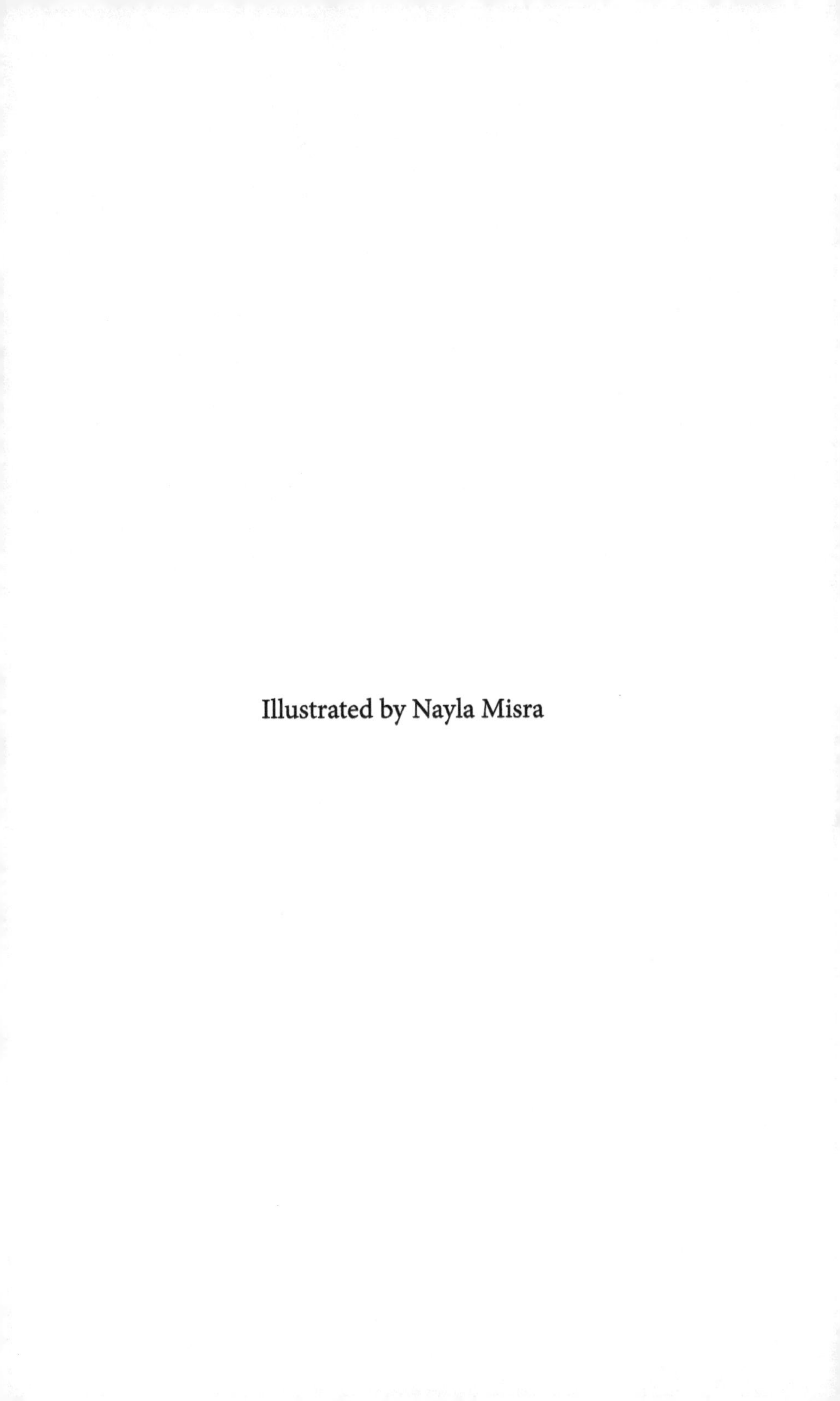

Illustrated by Nayla Misra

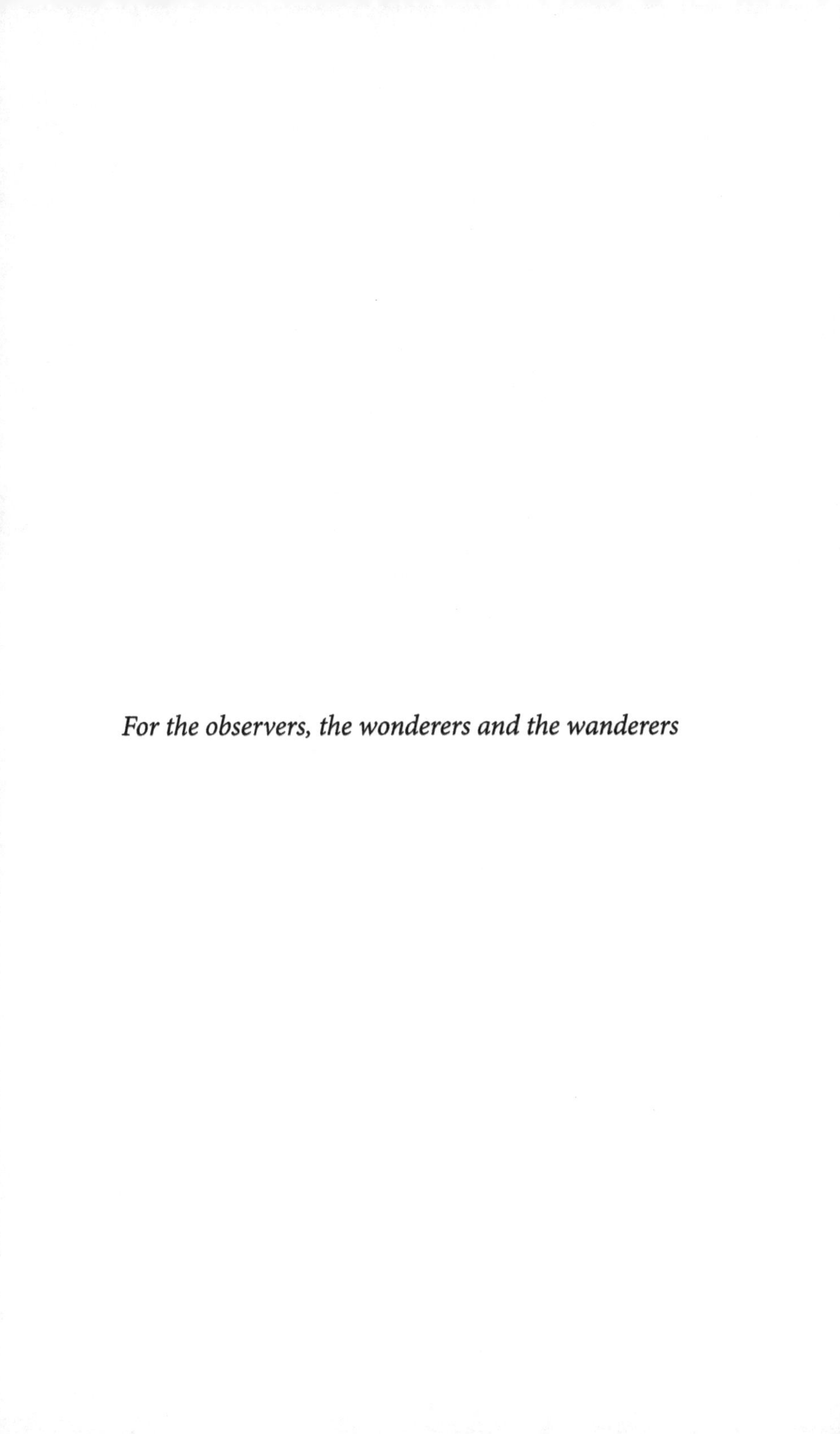

For the observers, the wonderers and the wanderers

CONTENTS

LOVE

Love will come to you

In its own time

not as droplets

But as a tide

It's easy to swim

But wouldn't it be mesmerising

for once

To Embrace as you sink

LIGHT

I asked the sun
Where he gets his light from
All he said was
It's a mixture of hope and happiness
He likes to shine upon us

It was then that I
could feel my own rays
Glowing inside of me
asking to be free

I could feel the warmth
That relies on my own ecstasy
sparking my soul
to the oblivious reality

Stars

Why then do we still look up at the stars

If not for hope

For peace

For a fulfilling company as one

that cannot be found on solid ground

And

In wonderment

of the World that could be

instead of only

What we are made to believe

DROPLETS

Find me where the rain is

Everywhere and all at once

Then watch as those droplets

Turn into tsunamis

Of tears

Of my patience

Of what I've become

REASONS?

We mostly think that
Most things in life demand a reason,
a purpose

But do you really need a reason
To look up at the sky and
take a breath
to remove your shoes and walk on the ticklish grass
And to feel the warmth even in the sunset

Or to smile at the people you love everyday
And give someone comfort through a warm embrace

Sometimes it's okay to just be happy
To not question everything
And just live in those little moments
That give you answers you never even asked for

And create whispers in your mind
to
Just.Keep.Going

BELONG

She belonged to a world where no one was forced to fit into a crowd

Where difference was praised

not caged

Where there was a place for each face

She belonged to a world where no one had to belong,

They could just be.

Words Unsaid

And so

She stopped replying

She knew

Not to waste her words

On those

Who have already been hurt

by themselves

Those who now wish to fill that void

through contention

Those who will never know

The victory

in words unsaid

LIVE

I think I'm starting to live a little
Starting to love living

But not because the sun lights up my room everyday
Rather because the stormy clouds await
outside my window
And there is a certain comfort I find in them
They understand me,
like a jeweller would a gem

I think I'm starting to live a little
But not because I suddenly don't make mistakes
Or don't cry every now and then
But because I am human,
And I have accepted it

I live to learn
And not to turn
away from
Challenges that have led me
To a growth with embrace

And it's when you stop waiting

for the moments of joy

Instead, start making them

That you truly know,

The sun will shine again

but

only after the storm

Which is beautiful

in its own form

SOMEONE

Maybe I am nothing more than

someone in a crowd

a droplet amongst oceans

A constellation passing by

Yet I'm grateful that I'm here

In a world full of possibilities

I've been given a chance to be

Someone

WORLD(S)

I closed my eyes

And escaped

To a world

Magical, mysterious, wondrous

I felt

Complete

Flying, floating, free

And I knew

This was the place of my dreams

I wouldn't say it wasn't real

For who are we to say

That ours is the only reality

When we are oblivious

To what may be

Being forced to see

restrictively

A place unlike any other
I wish in which I had stayed forever
Yet, there's only so far to travel
for the wanderer
Everyone must come out of
their world of wonder

As I open my eyes I still carry
That unplaced connection
Somewhere deep buried

In another dimension what could I have been?
With that unanswered question
I carry on
with my daily routine

But not without a hint of smile
The only constant I carry
From the other world

Nostalgia

I had a dream…

Skipping around
A game
Called hopscotch
So deeply rooted to the ground
Cycling in circles
Home was it?

Up and down I went
Trying to reach the sky
wind in my face
Swings they called it
Who knew?
A simple playground
Could mean so much

A dancer one day
A pirate the next
A singer, a superhero
whatever I dreamt

I was reading a story
'Fairytales' they called it
A gift as I open my eyes
"Yes, my birthday!"
Who knew
The true gift
was the excitement

They say it was childhood
It's all such a blur
Yet even this bittersweet feeling
Is enough
To keep me going

Memories, is it?

Me?

I can't put into words

How I'm losing a bit of myself

More and more everyday

My eyes can't see past

My own reflection

Only an allegory

Of the world's representation

And

The different versions of me

That aren't even mine…

sometimes everyone needs to sit back and reflect

what is really theirs?

Nonlinear

I can't see people

as clusters of matter

Organised into flesh and bone

Entering the world

Only to be controlled

What I do see

Is happiness and ecstasy

Individuals with their own pain

And journey

with their diverse souls

And stories

In the same way,

I can't accept a linear path to life

It isn't meant to be laid out

It shouldn't be set

"Never cross that line"

"Every goal must be met"

What I really want are moments

To hold

Smiles to capture

To be bold

To live every day like my story is being told

Maybe we could be nonlinear

somewhere in a faraway land

Where the excitement isn't endured

Where we aren't just flesh and bone

But free

to be something more

Signs & Sighs

Tree branches and leaves

Sunlight in a stream

Warmth embracing me

Like a bird's wings when they are free

Asking nothing in return

Hoping humans have learnt

The importance

of the sun and ferns

They continue to burn

A cold breeze passes by

As if nature just sighed

There's a reason we'll never learn

how to fly

For our toxic touch

has incinerated even the sky

A Reminder

I want to write you something
But maybe it won't be good enough
I want to draw you as a painting
but my hands won't heal from the cut
You gave me when I felt safe
When you saw me
as something you could replace
And yet

What you never saw coming
Was the end of my walks
And the beginning of a race

That I would always win
Because I *learned* how to run
when I was never able to catch up
With you

I learned your moves and your tricks

As I was passing by you

You never saw me again

only the footprints

I left behind

A sign

For all the steps you will now have to take

A reminder

of something you will now never replace.

HOME

The walk home
Was longer than expected
As the breeze brushed past my hair
And the drizzle of the rain went by
As I stared into the distance
In epiphanies of self

The walk home was longer than expected
Not because of the distance
Or the friction of the wind
But because of the resistance in my mind

How quickly it passes by
The time
When you don't notice

As I reached
the name-plate decorated gate
I looked back
To find the empty street
Challenging me to solitude versus company

Ignoring it

I entered home

Where I can find the comfort of both

My own time and

My family

LOOPS

I'm afraid

if I let myself feel

I won't stop

I'm afraid if I choose to choose

I'll miss out

I'm afraid

I might be stuck

in this endless loop

Forever

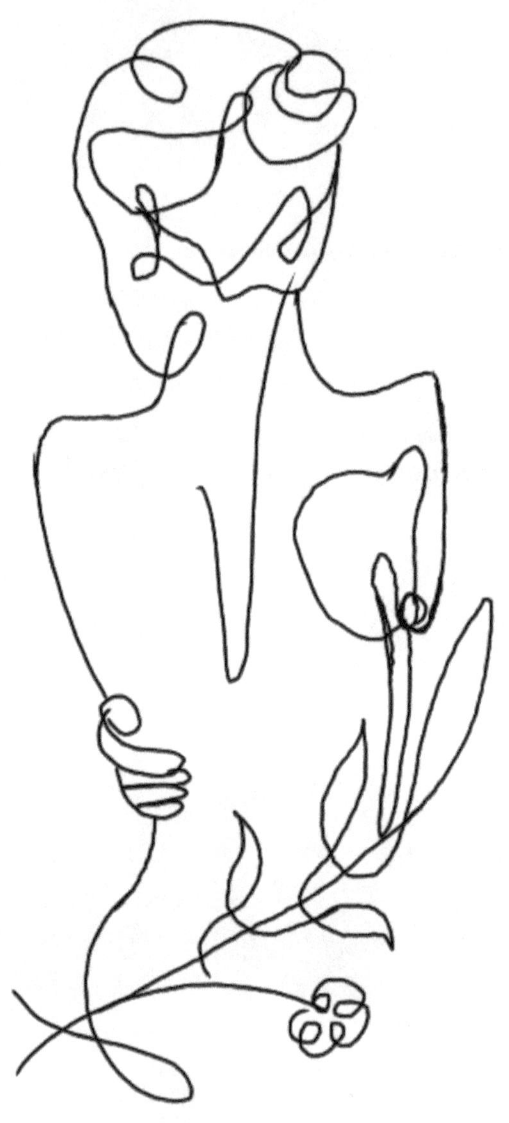

SHE

She is like the stars

Always there but hidden by the world

She is like a rose

Petals and thorns

her beauty and weapon

She is a mother, a sister, a daughter, a wife,

a figure, an inspiration

She is a

Woman

CRAZY FREE

When it rains
She doesn't hide away
She goes out and plays like a child
Soaking and jumping and being wild

When she reads
She doesn't see words
She sees worlds,
She giggles and laughs and cries
And then makes her own stories,
Which are never to be heard

When she dances
She doesn't wait around for others
She turns the music up
And twists and turns till her feet hurt

And when she is asked who she wants to be

She doesn't answer

For she knows they won't be able to see

She has always been a free spirit

Why should she now be concealed?

And so she is fine with being perceived

As crazy

She chooses memories over maybes

Discover

It is so easy, so static

For those who are noticed

to be found without effort by others

But it is oh so beautifully adventurous

To be lost,

To be unseen

and have the privilege to discover

Yourself

THE CLIMB

What a shame

She went

tumbling down those slopes

yet what pride

She felt

learning how to climb back up

A Poem

What is a poem

If not a song

That gives melody to the written word

Unspoken,

yet never unheard

BLACK & WHITE

Black and white
Is all I am
Is all I have ever been
To those who can't see colour
Black and white
Is what I'll remain
Merely an optical illusion
My dreams a mirage

What they'll never see
Is that even black and white
Is a combination and absorption of colours
So many different versions of me
Alas, Trapped
for they could never be free

So
Black and white
Is all I'll ever be

THE OTHER SIDE

In my writings

I usually try and stay positive

But that is only after I have tolerated

The whispers and stares and unnecessary glares

That have left me in despair

Yes I want to be optimistic

Even though my thoughts are scattered and dispersed

And it is I who has brought it

Upon myself

I'm an over thinker, not a decision maker

And every day I try to conceal it

Behind words, the other side of the mirror

I tell you this now

Because I want you to accept

the emotions that are harder to show

Just know

Sometimes you have to reach the eye of the cyclone

To find composure

and a steady flow

In the Nature

In the grass
She saw versions of herself
Wild, uncontrolled, annoying

In the moon
She saw her soul,
How it came alive
A few nights
How it dimmed
And the others sighed

In the river
She saw her mind
Going up and down with the tide
Her willpower like the current
You couldn't stop her if you tried

In the sky you could see her moods
Some colours so beautiful
others were dull, better eschewed

And that's where she found herself
In the nature, so intricately simple
Away from humankind
But never far enough to be unaffected
Alas,
forcing her to hide her different sides

I WANT...

I want peace
But I can't live without the thrill of it all

I want love
But it's an insatiable web
of unrequitedness

I want to live in a thousand worlds
But I can't even make it through this one

I want solitude
But I can't seem to be with myself

And lately
I don't think
I'll ever completely know
What I truly want

62 ✱ *The Ever-Growing Vine on My Window*

WHEN THE MUSIC PLAYS

And when the music plays

It doesn't hit her ears, it hits her soul

She feels an unworldly connection,

A memory that can't quite be placed

But it's there

Because she knows the music, and the music knows her

So she waits

Just like she does everyday

For a person who won't just look at her

But will see her

Someone who will know her without her having to say anything

Who will hit her soul, without any reasoning

"I'm always gonna love you."

"I'm always gonna love you too."

- La La Land

DANDELION

Sometimes I feel like a dandelion

Inexorably blown away

Maybe a little too easily

Never knowing where to go

Or how to stay

Free yet controlled by the wind

No destination, no place that awaits

Sometimes I feel like a dandelion

One moment I am still

The other I move through the breeze

Dancing past the trees,

Passing by the hills

Sometimes I feel like a dandelion

Ever so light

Growing with things that are more in sight

Yet never losing my shine

Don't scatter the pieces of me

I must always be pretty

Be easy with me

I am delicate

Yet

always a sight to see

But I know

Because I am a dandelion

You will never love me whole

Only the parts of me

You like to see

As I leave

As I get blown

far away, never again to be shown

Shattered

Shattered glass
Endless reflection of light
An amalgamation of different colours
only to show broken pieces of me
lying on the floor
my own vision a question

But then the truth is cleaned
Nothing broken should be kept
Hidden pieces of me
Have now been thrown away

Back to work
Where lies now reflect
in the illumination caused by light
In the eyes of people who can't see
what's inside
until more pieces break

And the mess

once again must be cleaned

But no one realises

It's never glued back together

But rather

it moves on as a pollutant

Now give me a thousand more years

to decompose

So that

I am forever gone

REMEMBRANCE

I am eloquent enough
To write a song
But when it comes to you
I somehow wander off

My mind freezes
My heart stops
As I remember your wheedling words
Fuelling my altruistic thoughts

Where am I now?
I was never like this.
I wish I had stopped
Seeing your apathy
as an exhilarating fit

But how could I have

I was blind

For now that I have opened my eyes

I don't see you anymore

I only see me

Standing alone in a land I envisaged for us both

Yet somehow I feel relieved

That I didn't turn into a glacier

And made my way

into the open sea

THE AFTERMATH

The storms are getting harsher

The tide is getting stronger

The wave is leaping higher

Hold on, dear, do that desire

For the sun is also only appreciated

Once the seeping cold

has showed you its worth

So you must believe

that when the time comes,

You will stop the run

You will face the world

and it will not tell you anything

Rather it will see that you made it

It will realise that

You're higher

than any wave

Stronger

than any tide

and

Harsher

than any storm.

BEAUTY

And as the world ended

Beauty was finally appreciated

Skies seemed to be all

The eyes would ever need

Phones were not picked up

To capture and store

things materialistically

Money seemed to have no use

What was held on to

was people, their love and memories

Pure, unfiltered, and true

and so Beauty

came sudden, unexpected

In anything and everything

A living message

Just as the world ended

Deep Down

Deep down
Aren't we all just humans
Leaving behind our ethnicity, caste, creed, race, gender
Sometimes we all want to surrender

Deep down
Don't we all just want a hug
A few kind words passed
That make it seem like humanity
might just be of worth

Deep down
We all want to be loved
For while there are things you do for a living
There is love
That makes life feel like it's breathing

Don't forget to make someone happy today.

You won't even realise it,

but a smile on someone else's face

can turn into your very own happiness instead.

MEMORIES

I don't know what I'd do
without these memories I make
The love that I gain
and the photos to frame
Live in my heart forever

I'll forget them never
The times we went through together
A treasure tethered
That I can open whenever

And it is then that I know
Looking at the moments we have sowed,
There are so many more to grow
And to hold on to,
Forevermore

SPARKS

And how the spark ignited a wish,

she did not know

But when the fireworks exploded

she saw so many more sparks

waiting,

for her

Fire

DIFFERENT

Only because you're different

Doesn't mean you're not enough

Or that you don't belong

It just means you'll sing your own song

And make it through,

Without their definitions

of rights and wrongs

The Moon

Be the moon that draws the tide higher

Make them rise, make them seen

Just when they think they've lost

their self-esteem

Pull them back up,

Become the shoulder on which they can lean

And when the day comes and the sun shines brighter

You will still be there in their hearts,

Hidden

but never unseen

Fires in the Forest

A ferocious fire

Amidst the serene forest

Spread like the wings of a butterfly

It was beautiful

All catastrophes are

"Don't extinguish it", she whispered

For it was the only way

Nature could at last scream

Everlasting Works

And so the creator

Looked behind at their own work

Which now came to an end

But left behind

Beautiful Beginnings

FOREVER

Forever with grace I fall

Forever in solitude I walk

With pride I stand tall

Away, so far away, from all thoughts

Running, pacing, turning, not one stop

You'll never find me, I don't linger, don't care

About your shaming talks

I'll be lost in the trees,

camouflaging, dissolving, unbridling

Till I'm gone,

Forever. Never again to be crossed.

MAGIC

Sparkle your life

With magic

Like pixie dust and enchanted forests

Let glitter spread,

for once it is,

It's quite hard to collect

Like the ones in storybooks,

The pirates, the princes, the moon lake, and Captain Hook

Let your imagination run wild,

Just as when you were a child

I miss those times

A vicarious world, allowing for fascinating foresights

Sometimes I still dream

Of magical carpets, lanterns, lost slippers,

dazzling dresses

Castles that would seem endless,

Battles passed in a sunset

And always I hope,

That that world

is so much closer than it seems

So I sparkle my life with magic

And realise that just letting my imagination

run wild

Brings me closer to all the places

I want to find

Magic spreads everywhere,

There's fog, mist, stars, fairy lights

I'm finally *transported to another time*

MOMENTS

The beauty of living
is moments
And the beauty of moments
is that they are so unexpected,
random

There is no better feeling
than to find those moments
And capture them in your heart
To live fully when you get the chance

And it is then
in that nonsensical manner
In which you laugh with your friends
or gaze out the window
or spend time by yourself
That some bit of life
starts making sense
"The best things in life, the very best things,
happen unexpectedly."
- Mamma Mia! Here We Go Again

SILENCE

Silence

Is nothing but

The aftermath

of the chaos

Too much noise caused

PETALS & THORNS

I was so focused

on growing my Petals

that I became incognisant

of the Thorns that protected me

IMPERFECT WORDS

She used to get speechless

Struggling to find the perfect words,

An incomplete thought

But now she's grateful

that she can see power

in her imperfect words

Thoughts that have now turned

into meanings

Words

that are now a feeling

LIGHT IN THE DARK

And just the way

The dark highlights

The moon's ineffable beauty

These tough times will inevitably exhort you

To live fully

in those perfect moments

that await you

remember, even the moon doesn't always shine bright

PRETTY

Pretty
Just not the kind you expect
In the cascading, repeating patterns of trees
But rather the intricate, unique design
of its branches

Pretty
Just not the kind everyone wants
The brightest like the stars
But rather with scars
Like the only moon in the sky

Pretty
Just not perfect
Not the kind of beauty that everyone sees
But the kind that a few find

Beauty
That lasts
Not lingers

FEELINGS

Today it rained
Ever so fiercely
On my window pane
It suddenly came,
The slight drizzle
That turned into a harsh splatter of sound,
of petrichor familiarness

And as the heavy beads washed across my face
I felt lighter than ever

Then the wind and water whispered in my ear
You can cry with me dear
Be it tears
Of happiness or joy
You can release the drizzles
That you feared
Would turn into disastrous thunderstorms

Until you realised that

you love watching the black sky appear

in its many forms

That maybe letting go of your pain

Will make someone else feel

that theirs is not vain

And so while watching the thunderstorm

an understanding was passed

through a suppressed song,

Emotions are what has given life its meaning

all along

"Close your eyes. Now feel."- Barbie '23

THE ONE

You're my The One

The One I go to when I'm drowning

You don't pull me up, you let me sink in,

then lift me up

You show me how to be tough

and yet provide me with a warm embrace

in your hug

You're my The One

The One I can be crazy around

Not half me, parts I mostly conceal

But the whole me,

all the parts I never thought

would be free

You're my The One

The One I'll share all my troubles with

The One I'll cry with and laugh

The One who knows me enough to listen like you know nothing
at all

You're The One

my sun, my comfort, my power

catching me when I fall,

raising me even higher

Stars

Why then do we look up at the stars

If not for hope

for peace

For a fulfilling company as one

that cannot be found on solid ground

and

in wonderment

of the world that could be

Instead of only

what we are made to believe

She'll be Fine

I'll be fine

she said

As she counted droplets

on the pages of her book

Some hers

Some the rain's

that seemed to understand her

I'll be fine

she roared

Escaping the room full of whispers

And fools

who would one day know

what was coming for them all along

I'll be fine
she shouted
But she never was
She never did say I'm fine

Yet she knew that one day she should feel it
better than most

That one day she'll be the
best version of herself she can

And then she'll ask them questions
they can never answer in the present
But only seek for
in the future

The Art of Noticing

How grateful I feel

for the art of noticing

In a world where time is just a measure

and busy days pass by

Noticing or even to be noticed

Is to become the Passenger

and not just a passer by

EVER-GROWING

The vine on my window grows
Through winter, storms, sun and hail it holds
Creeping up on the glass,
forever bold

It harbours flowers, birds, leaves,
A whole ecosystem within one creeper
Nourishing free

I watch as the gardener cuts its branches
Refraining it from going out of reach
And yet the next day it has grown back again
Untouched, ivies flourishing in the scorching sun

I watch as the vine grows more dense than ever
Beautiful than before, like it's been reborn,
even after all the challenges it has foregone
Silently suggesting,
Maybe it's not why they cut your wings
Maybe it's about how you will reform

So I continue watching everyday

How the vine creeps up to my window pane

Always aiming to go just a little higher,

unafraid of reaching the sky,

Spreading wherever it sees a way

And suddenly I hear a part of me say

Let them cut you open as they may

Let them try and yank you to the ground

Preventing you from being found

All will be in vain

For whichever path you now take

As long as your roots stay the same

You will always find your escape

And like the vine on your window

You will stay

Ever-growing,

never to be caged

ACKNOWLEDGEMENTS

With deepest gratitude to:

My mom and dad, who always encouraged me to continue writing, even when I had given up on my talent. This book wouldn't be possible without your constant support.

My grandmother and my brother, who probably never understood what I was writing yet always praised my poems.

All my teachers, who pushed me to my best limit and imparted the knowledge I needed to today be a published writer.

My friends and Insta followers who have always motivated me to write more and bestowed so much love for my work.

And to you, who has shown yet another form of support by reading my first ever book.

Thank you.